THE WOUNDED SOLDIER

The Wounded Soldier
Copyright © 2022 by Joseph Karasanyi

Published in the United States of America
ISBN   Paperback: 978-1-959761-09-9
ISBN   eBook: 978-1-959761-10-5

All rights reserved. No part of this publication may be reproduced, stored in a retrieval system or transmitted in any way by any means, electronic, mechanical, photocopy, recording or otherwise without the prior permission of the author except as provided by USA copyright law.

The opinions expressed by the author are not necessarily those of ReadersMagnet, LLC.

ReadersMagnet, LLC
10620 Treena Street, Suite 230 | San Diego, California, 92131 USA
1.619. 354. 2643 | www.readersmagnet.com

Book design copyright © 2022 by ReadersMagnet, LLC. All rights reserved.

Cover design by Kent Gabutin
Interior design by Dorothy Lee

THE WOUNDED SOLDIER

*(The Wounded Gospel Minister Vs.
The Wounded Marine Soldier)*

JOSEPH KARASANYI

ReadersMagnet, LLC

TABLE OF CONTENTS

Introduction 7

The Similarity Between Gospel Minister And Soldier 9

    Same Leadership

    Same Purpose

    Same Principle

The Danger Of Making Ourselves Judges Over Our Fellowmen 19

Wounds That Serve The Devil's Purpose 26

    Physical Battle

    The Principal of Battle

    The Gate Wounds

    They Need Unity

Our Heavenly Father Wants To Erase Your Disgrace 36

You Matter In The Eyes Of Your Heavenly Father 48

The Divine Antidote 59

INTRODUCTION

Both the wounded gospel minister and the wounded soldier, though from different forces, work and do similar jobs, albeit for different masters. Both follow similar principles in the mode of work. Both of them have their different command hierarchies where they get orders as they do their job.

Both always have to dress in uniformed combat gear given to them by higher authority, and they do have orders from their high command to follow and obey. Both the gospel minister and soldier must have a leader in the charge of each unit, and for both, there has to be one major principal from which they take orders. They must obey the orders from your high command and disciples. And for those who have ever worked for both parties, you would know that the gospel minister and soldier both obey orders without question.

Both have enemies, even though they fight different wars. Indeed, they both have and use weapons to fight. Consequently, they get wounded. They can't avoid the wounded ones in their numbers, and sometimes, some die of serious wounds. Both, when they die, are carried by six men accompanying the coffin.

Like all casualties, the wounded are helped by comrades on the same battlefront, who, if possible, take them to the hospital or sickbay and try their best to ensure they survive the wounds inflicted by the enemy. Both the evangelist and soldier follow a similar cardinal principle: they have to obey all orders from their high command; the basic tenet is to cover and protect one's colleagues and to be in the spirit of unity and oneness for them to coordinate their activities well.

In the same spirit, the wounded are evacuated from the enemy frontline. The soldiers must fight, but also cover the wounded friend until he gets medical help and ensure that he can survive and recover from enemy-inflicted wounds.

Incidentally, when it comes to the wounded gospel minister, his friends or fellow ministers forget the code of unity and don't cover their fellow minister, and instead of the good fight aimed at helping their fellow minister to recover from wounds, they cover him with negative publicity, and if he doesn't die quickly, they want to bury him alive. They dishearten him by harshly judging him, blaming him, and even cursing him. We don't see anywhere they treat wounded gospel ministers, no sickbay for them, and no hospital for gospel ministers to be treated to recovery. Everybody turns against them. With all their wounds, they eventually succumb to moral and spiritual death.

This book is made to create a sickbay or hospital for the wounded minister who has not yet died from the fatal wounds. As a minister, get this book today; praise God, for you can live again! You won't die before your time. Your Master has not given up on you, and He is coming back soon. Evidently, we all agree that soldiers and gospel ministers have similar missions and similar job hazards but different treatments when wounded.

(1)

THE SIMILARITY BETWEEN GOSPEL MINISTER AND SOLDIER

Wounded Soldier

Wounded Gospel Minister

Let us have an in-depth look into the similarity between a marine soldier and a gospel minister. We are also going to see what the word of God says about wounded ones. It is where we are going to find out the truth about these two, soldiers and ministers, who serve in different kingdoms but with the same way of serving their kingdoms.

They have the same kind of leadership. Both have their high command as center of their leadership, which has a defined structure and responsibilities. Both have the same principles to keep their discipline and obey orders from their leaders.

The army commander, has all his orders from top to bottom. Jesus, our Lord, said to his disciples and all believers to obey his command which comes from the top, from His Father to the lowest person. That is the same with the soldier who has to take orders from higher authorities of the army. As the soldier takes orders from higher authorities, the gospel minister has to go by the orders and command from above.

Both have different tiers of leadership and channels to top leaders, but all keep order from an above authority in everything they have to do. They have dressing codes and similar codes of conduct according to orders given by the authority. The believers have a dressing code as revealed in Ephesians 6:10-11, where they are told to be strong, dress up in full armor like soldiers, and stand by ready for war.

This shows us that every believer and every minister is required to have a dressing code just like a soldier. He has to put on his full physical and spiritual uniform and will thus be identified as God's minister, just as a soldier's country will be known from his uniform. The word of God says:

"Finally, be strong in the Lord and in his mighty power.
Put on the full armor of God, so that you can
take your stand against the devil's schemes.
For our struggle is not against flesh and blood,
but against the rulers, against the authorities,
against the powers of this dark world and against
the spiritual forces of evil in the heavenly realms."

For the soldier has to be in full gear for a battle, and they are ready to go to battle with a single purpose: to fight the good fight and win. He will be thanked and recognized, decorated and promoted. He will be called a hero! Similarly, every believer or gospel minister is required to put on the gospel armor and fight (Eph 6:12-13) until the victory is won for the Lord!

In the same spirit, a soldier fights tooth and nail to win the war and defend his country until the foe is vanquished and his country flag flies high. The believer or gospel minster should always be ready to fight a good fight and come home to be given a crown in glory. Like the Apostle Paul, he should confidently say:

> *"I have fought a good fight, I have won the race,*
> *but most importantly, I have kept the faith."*
> *1 Tim. 4:17*

Both have known leadership and principles governing their missions. They don't do what they want but what the one who send them commands wants. They go by their leaders' plan and purpose. Both the gospel ministers and soldiers face battles and get the supplies from higher authority. Our Lord Jesus, as our commander in chief, gave us fundamental orders:

> [15] *"If you love me, keep my commands.*
> [16] *And I will ask the Father,*
> *and he will give you another advocate*
> *to help you and be with you forever.*
> [17] *This is my command: love each other."*
> *John 15:15-17*

And as we see in scriptures, God is our supplier of all our needs. It is the same way the soldiers get their supply from their high command, as revealed in Philippians.

> [19] *"And my God will meet all your needs according*
> *to the riches of his glory in Christ Jesus.*
> [20] *To our God and Father be glory for ever and ever. Amen"*
> *Ph. 4:19-20*

At the battlefront, the high authorities require soldiers to observe the unity and oneness that results in the strength needed to win battles and, eventually, the war. Unity of purpose is a necessity for both soldiers and preachers. It means the same in these different camps. It is the reason why Jesus Christ our Lord calls us to be one, as He and His Father are one.

> *³⁴ "A new command I give you: Love one another.*
> *As I have loved you, so you must love one another.*
> *³⁵ By this, everyone will know that you are my disciples, if you love one another."*
> *John 13:34-36*

The apparent point in this similarity between minister and soldier is that both use weapons to fight; therefore, both get wounded and are potential casualties on the battlefield. Although they have different battlefields and use different weapons, both get wounded. Injuries and causalities can be found on both battlefields.

Both gospel minister and military soldier have many things in common. The only difference between them is that the soldiers on the frontline have a unity and orders to take care of the wounded and sick and treat them. At the battlefront, soldiers fight and risk their lives to save the wounded. If the wounded is unable to walk, they will carry him and will risk their life in the process, as they are fight to rescue the wounded comrade. They try their best, not only to rescue him, but also to ensure he does not die. They use all comforting and encouraging words to the wounded soldier, like: "don't worry, you will be fine"; "it's okay, we will take you back home"; "it's fine"; and, "we are here with you." All aim at trying to make the wounded feel safe. Ultimately, if the soldier can't make it, he will at least die in kind hands. Remember, soldiers do all this not only to save a comrade but to save a wounded soldier in total obedience of the high command and those in authority.

The Wounded Soldier

In the soldiers' spirit of obedience to seriously take orders from their commanding officers lies the source of success.

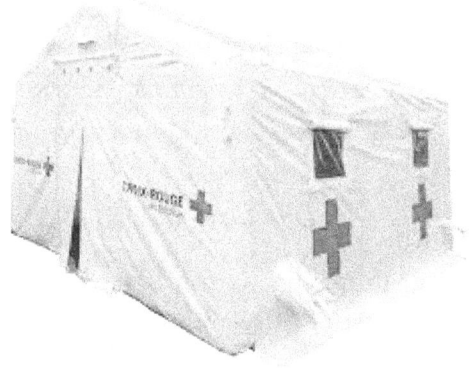

The bitter reality is that when the believer and gospel minister get wounded on the frontline, they don't have anybody to take care of them. No one carries the injured to from the frontline to the hospital, and there no soothing words of encouragement. Even though the word of God advises the church in Gal. 6:1-2 to behave exactly like the army to those wounded on duty, the orders have fallen on deaf ears like the proverbial seeds that fell on rock. The word of God tells us to carry each other's burdens, to handle gently those are wounded among us, and to give special care, love, and compassion and fight hard to ensure none is lost. Unfortunately, as the believers, we are doing the opposite. Instead, we take sides and apportion blame and judge the wounded. Instead of the caring and encouraging that soldiers do, we accuse and blame, hit, and bombard our wounded brothers or sisters to spiritual demise. We forget that this is the time a wounded minister or believer needs help even more. He needs help from fellow ministers more than ever before. He needs encouragement and more fellowship to reconcile and treat his moral and spiritual wounds. But what the believers and ministers do to him is also a breach of the order from their high command. They contravene the laws they are supposed to defend. They break the greatest commandment: "Love your neighbor as you love yourself!"

As the word of God says in Gal. 6:1,

"Brothers and sisters, if someone is caught in a sin, you who live by the Spirit should restore that person gently. But watch yourselves, or you also may be tempted. 2 Carry each other's burdens, and in this way, you will fulfill the law of Christ."

This is a profound command: to stand in the gap, to cover our fellow wounded brothers and sisters. This is the tall order from our high command to have a special office of caring for those who are wounded among us.

We all can see as believers and ministers that we are governed by the same principle as the military: to cover and be there for one another, especially in times of crisis. The word of God instructs us to treat the wounded or sick with love and gentility and, where necessary, pay for the hospital bills like the Good Samaritan did. We are charged to restore the person, and this means that when we deal with the wounded with careless attitudes, we can cause more wounds, more pain, and more problems. What happens to the wounded among us is sad because we have found that nobody is ready to cover a fellow minister the way the military treats the wounded comrades.

As we saw before, once one is wounded, fellow believers and ministers, instead of carrying them from the frontline to safety, they judge and condemn him, use hurting words (like "shame on you," "fake minister," etc.), and storm him with curses and disheartening words, literally digging his grave while he is still alive, ready to bury him then and there. They forget the code of unity and oneness which is a requirement on the earthly battle field; they all forget regardless of the name of church or denomination they belong. They forget that with a Christian background, they have the same enemy and same master.

Sadly, they forget that the enemy who has hit a fellow minister is the same enemy who is prepared to devour them all. On the contrary, the military knows the principle that the enemy who has hit a colleague is the same enemy who is coming back for you. It is sad that the world soldier knows this principle better than those who call themselves the children of God. When soldiers fight to save a colleague, when they carry him on their shoulders to ensure his survival, they know the same enemy who has hit their friend is coming back with the same weapon for them. Lamentably, while the soldiers are rescuing a wounded colleague, believers and ministers are blaming the fellow minister, judging and condemning him as they turn away from him and go away leaving nature to take its course. The wounded minister is isolated and is left alone in pain from his spiritual and body wounds. Most ministers don't survive. They give up, keep quiet, and crawl away to hide from the cruel public, living by the grace of God, who hates sin but loves the sinner. The discouragement forces some ministers to feel that they are no longer worthy to be called ministers any more. They are demoralized and spiritually defeated.

The above is fundamentally serious. The more the believers and ministers continue to behave that way, the more the body of Christ loses the battle. With believers who behave like Pharisees and count themselves to be the most righteous, the enemy must be rejoicing. The believer or minister whose job is to judge others is doing exactly what the enemy wants. Now, when Satan, the enemy, finds out that many are wounded, this makes him declare victory and be happy for his progress.

When the Lord Jesus demonstrated the value of one sinner saved, He said that one soul repenting makes all heaven to rejoice, meaning that one soul lost makes all of heaven sad. The image is a miserable one indeed, when one soul backslides and is down with spiritual wounds and is out of grace. This is what the bible demonstrates in the parables of the lost sheep and the old woman's coin. Our lord doesn't want to lose even a single soul.

> *[1] "Now the tax collectors and sinners were all gathering around to hear Jesus. [2] But the Pharisees and the teachers of the law muttered, 'This man welcomes sinners and eats with them.' [3] Then Jesus told them this parable: [4] 'Suppose one of you has a hundred sheep and loses one of them. Doesn't he leave the ninety-nine in the open country and go after the lost sheep until he finds it? [5] And when he finds it, he joyfully puts it on his shoulders [6] and goes home. Then he calls his friends and neighbors together and says,*
> *Rejoice with me; I have found my lost sheep. [7] I tell you that in the same way, there will be more rejoicing in heaven over one*

sinner who repents than over ninety-nine righteous persons who do not need to repent.
⁸ Or suppose a woman has ten silver coins and loses one. Doesn't she light a lamp, sweep the house and search carefully until she finds it? ⁹ And when she finds it, she calls her friends and neighbors together and says,
Rejoice with me; I have found my lost coin. ¹⁰ In the same way, I tell you, there is rejoicing in the presence of the angels of God over one sinner who repents."
Luke 15:1-10

It is very sad that up to today, we who claim to belong to the body of Christ have not yet found out this secret of the devil so that we can work out to forge unity and oneness as we face the battle. We have quickly and sadly forgotten that we have one common enemy as the body of Christ and children of God. Today, we have thousands of men and women of God who are spiritually handicapped, moving in spiritual wheelchairs, while others have suffered beyond recovery due to the blows on the frontline and the mistreatment and unfair judgments which serve to mess up their calling and ministries.

This book is essentially a helping hand to everybody who was wounded in any away. We hope that it is going to help you to work on your situation and soothe your wounds because the life must continue although the war is waging on continually. The most important factor in this war is that God still counts on you to fight, win, and come out as a victor.

Therefore, even though your wounds are still very open and painful, they are going to heal and leave no scars. The blood of Jesus Christ is still active and healing up to today, even before he comes again.

(2)

THE DANGER OF MAKING OURSELVES JUDGES OVER OUR FELLOWMEN

Many ministers are nursing wounds caused by bad and damaging verdicts passed on them by those talented at condemning others. The lies and comments from false judges are part of the weapons of destruction from the devil's arsenal used to destroy the body of Christ. That is why we start with the issue of judgment as a first arrow in the devil's bow. Woe to them that have mastered the art of pointing fingers!

For church ministers, being judgmental is a very important character flaw we don't usually talk about, yet it is one of the devil's strongest weapons that he uses to crush relationships, destroy trust among brothers, and in most cases, cause never-ending conflicts among families and believers. It is through the judging of others that many get seriously wounded. As it is written, the reckless words pierce like sword.

> *[18]* *"The words of the reckless pierce like swords, but the tongue of the wise brings healing."*
> **Proverbs 12:18**

In most cases, when people get any negative information or stories, they don't care how the message or information can be a subtle and dangerous tool Satan uses to mount character destruction through hatred and conflict. When people engage in judging others, the resulting holier-than-thou atmosphere needs a mere spark to set it on fire.

For everything good God created, the devil tries to create a counterfeit to deceive the world. At its best, the word "judgment" is indeed adjudication, which means the evaluation of evidence to make a decision. Judgment is also the ability to make considered decisions. Therefore, to a minister already wounded by the cruel circumstances dictated by the nature of his job, it is better to come close and evaluate the situation before we put him on the weighing machine of success and failure. In an attempt to carry judgment against a brother, we fall in with fake justice to add salt onto the wound.

More often than not, the person you are blaming needs some help which you can afford without being judgmental. That is why anything you say or do before you find out the truth might put you in a trap because you could become a missile in the hand of the devil as he tries to destroy the Church of Christ. In a normal court, a judge always asks for more evidence which helps him to pass judgment. However, among the children of God in our community, most don't foresee how dangerous our kangaroo court judgment is to fellow believers. And this is the main reason the wounded ministers deteriorate from bad to worse.

There are some potentially good ministers who have been consciously or unconsciously destroyed by fellow ministers because of the judging mentality that breeds demoralization and discouragement. Unfortunately, this kind of judgment is carried out by our fellow ministers or our friends, or even co-workers. Many have examples and can cite many once fruitful ministries, and even churches, where the Spirit of God ministered to many that have lost out because the minister was fatally wounded and the whole ministry had collapsed. Some ministries died and are no longer in existence while others are out to join others on the dunghill of history. That is the secret weapon in the hands of the devil. He knows that once the minister is aggrieved, the ministry gets wounded as well. That is why if no one cares, the ministry ends up going down, becomes weaker and weaker, and ultimately falls into oblivion. Very sad indeed!

Let us use this opportunity to ponder on this concern where a minister of the gospel commits the fundamental error of judging a fellow minister. This is for any minister at any level and from any denomination. When you speak evil against any minister of the gospel, you are not extinguishing the light from that man or woman of God, but you are busy bringing total darkness where people were enjoying light from Christ the King. Wherever you utter these negative words, you put the name of the Lord your God to shame. Before the minister is put to shame, the same words hit hundreds of weak members of that church or ministry who backslide and are irredeemably lost. For this, many will pay the price!

Let those forewarned be forearmed. If you are a minister who has been at the helm of judging others, you need to face that truth and humble yourself before God and ask forgiveness before you come face to face with what God says about making ourselves judges over our fellowmen. It is more dangerous to the judge than the judged!

When we look into God's word about what He says when we judge others, we find out that God will deal harshly with those who engage in this fatal error. The book of Romans talks about God's righteous judgment. It says:

"You, therefore, have no excuse,
you who pass judgment on someone else,
for at whatever point you judge another,
you are condemning yourself,
because you who pass judgment do the same things.
Now we know that God's judgment against
those who do such things is based on truth.
So when you, a mere human being,
pass judgment on them and yet do the same things,
do you think you will escape God's judgment?"
Romans 2:1-3

The scripture tells us plainly how judging others has dire consequences. Think about the chaos you would be in if all people that you judged were given chance to judge you. What if you sadly discover that in condemning them, you actually condemned yourself? Don't you think you would be in worse shape than those you judged? It is written that for God so loved the world, his mercy abounds.

"For God so loved the world that he gave his one and only Son,
that whoever believes in him shall not perish but have eternal
life."
John 3:16

In God's plan, He doesn't want to see his people perish, but your judgment condemns them. The scripture shows us how much God loves his people, and it puts us at the same level as people equal before Him. No big minister or small minister, no master and no slave - all are equal before the Lord. Our God does not measure greatness with what we see around us. We are equal, but the Lord gives us a big or small responsibility according to His perfect plan.

The word of God is telling us that each one has to account to God, whereby each one will have to present his case to God. That is the reason why when our fellow minister falls or is wounded, one should not judge or condemn him. It is not your day to rejoice. This is so because our God expects us to be our brother's keeper; hence, come to his rescue and try our best to work hard for his survival and recovery because we are one in Christ.

As we continue to see the word of God and what He says about judging others, we find out that it is a bid deal with God, but because of sinful ignorance, most people keep on judging others without thinking deeply about it. They take it easy without discerning the consequences. It is time we changed our attitude in how we treat each other in the body of Christ.

10 You, then, why do you judge your brother or sister[a]? Or why do you treat them with contempt? For we will all stand before God's judgment seat. It is written:

> *"As surely as I live,' says the Lord,*
> *'every knee will bow before me;*
> *every tongue will acknowledge God.'*
> *So then, each of us will give an account of ourselves to God."*
> *Romans 14:10-12*

Therefore, before you rise up against your fellow minister with cruel judgment, remember that you will account before God. You may find that you are carrying more baggage than these you are judging, guiltier, and in need of forgiveness. Always, before you attack those wounded in battles, first put yourself in their shoes and try to carry their burden as if it is yours. From that point of view, you can think about praying for them and forgive them. Since you have the same enemy, you never know; what has happened to your fellow minister can happen to you tomorrow. As they say, don't laugh at those who slide and fall, for there are more slippery grounds ahead!

More so, the scriptures warn us about the danger we put ourselves in as we judge others. This is the reason - if you are among the ministers who judge and mistreat others, destroying them with your judgment, please face that truth inside your heart and ask God for forgiveness before it is too late. My friend, you have no other way out of this trap. Because as it is written, you will be treated as you treat others. The standard you use in judging others is the same by which you will be the judged, and you will indeed be found guilty. Such are the consequences of engaging in the suicidal game of judging others. When we look in book of Matthew, we find a profound word of God: "Do not Judge." It is clearly as it is said:

"Do not judge, or you too will be judged.
For in the same way you judge others, you will be judged, and
with the measure you use,
it will be measured to you."
Matthew 7:1-2

THE PROFANITY OF JUDGING OTHERS

Some people do judge others through pride, others serve the spirit of self-righteousness, while others don't care at all about who gets hurt by their disheartening judgment. They are indeed sadists who derive pleasure from other people's suffering. Because the callous nature of this so-called judgment destroys the body of Christ, it should be avoided at all costs. It is thus said again in the Gospel of Luke:

> *"Do not condemn others,*
> *or it will all come back against you.*
> *Forgive others and you will be forgiven."*
> *Luke 6:37*

Therefore, we should be very careful not to judge, but consider what the word of God said about this situation because if we continue doing what we have been doing after knowing this truth, there will be no excuse.

(3)

WOUNDS THAT SERVE THE DEVIL'S PURPOSE

It is indeed clear your wounds serve the devil's purpose very well. Your weakness is his strength. Since we are on a battlefield and fighting with the enemy who comes with an order to kill and destroy, by all means, the wounded and dead will be many. It is therefore a matter of urgency to be on standby. The bible says

> *¹⁰ "The thief comes only to steal and kill and destroy;*
> *I have come that they may have life,*
> *and have it to the full. ¹¹ "I am the good shepherd.*
> *The good shepherd lays down his life for the sheep."*
> *John 10:10-11*

There is no joke. The above gives us the whole picture of what our enemy plans and his purpose of killing and destroying everybody in this same battle.

This time, we are going to focus on the wounded gospel ministers since we know that the soldiers within their structure have had this problem solved and that they know how to deal with the challenges that face the wounded among them. This time is for any gospel minister in any area of God's work or ministry who was wounded and those still on the frontline who may be wounded tomorrow. We need to take care of you before you lose the last spiritual breath. God still needs you back on your duty, and the body of Christ needs you in these last days when the laborers are few.

The fact that the scriptures talk about the abundance of the harvest and the scarcity of harvesters is the main reason why you are needed, not as a judge but because you are designed to be among the workers to gather the harvest for the Master. And the word continues to tell us to pray to the Lord for more workers but not to discourage the few already in the field. Before He assigns more work, those who are already sent just need to rise up and be back at work because there in our area, the harvest is ready, waiting for us to act.

> *[37]"Then he said to his disciples, 'The harvest is plentiful but the workers are few. [38] Ask the Lord of the harvest, therefore, to send out workers into his harvest field.'"*
> *Matthew 9:37-38*

As we saw in the army, they have a medic department who dresses the wounds of the wounded soldiers and a healing sickbay where they can take care of every wounded soldier to be treated and healed. Therefore, we are going to focus on the wounded gospel minister, and this book is a healing dose for the wounded minister. As a wounded minister, when you have the opportunity to read this book, it is going to dress your wounds, and the healing will take place from inside your heart. And it will change your attitude about yourself, so have confidence knowing that someone has already paid the price.

The Wounded Soldier

To the devil, your wounds are the flag of success he raises when you are wounded. He achieves his objectives and goals when you bite each other like insects in a bottle that bite each other instead of the bottle in which they are imprisoned. The bible reveals this as the character and personality of the devil who came to kill and destroy.

The great encouragement is our Lord Jesus, who went through more torture, and His wounds are far much more than what we are able to bear. The bible illustrates the physical pain and mental anguish Jesus suffered. He had bruises from head to the foot. I don't know how many bruises you have on your body, but certainly Jesus had more all over his body and deep in his heart. To compound the tragedy, he endured a painful crown of thorns! By God's grace, Jesus' wounds were so many so that they can restore us, and that is the reason we are going to be healed willy-nilly.

Long before Jesus was born, Isaiah prophesied about the wounds of our Lord Jesus and all the pain of his stripes:

> *"But he was wounded for our transgressions, _*
> *he was bruised for our iniquities: _*
> *the chastisement of our peace was upon him; _*
> *and with his stripes, we are healed.*
> *All we like sheep have gone astray; _*
> *we have turned everyone to his own way; _*
> *and the Lord hath laid on him the iniquity of us all."*
> *Isaiah 53:5, 6_*

We see that our Lord Jesus went through all these wounds so that you and me could get encouraged when we get wounded by our enemies.

Verse 5 explains that Jesus was wounded for our transgressions and was bruised for our iniquities so that when we are wounded, we may know Him as the healer of all our wounds. That is what He meant when he said that by his stripes, we are healed. Therefore, my friend, if you were wounded in any way, you are not alone, and there is provision for your healing because God's word is still alive and active when he said that by his stripes, we are healed.

Our Lord Jesus was wounded, but remember he had no sin, but many people in authority judged and pronounced him guilty. They knew about his innocence but went ahead and killed him. That is why you should keep faith in yourself even when everybody accuses and condemns you.

Most times, we don't deserve the harsh treatment and the wounds that come with them. You had nothing to do with the cause of your wounds. Indeed, someone is to blame. You are paying the price of something you didn't commit. Your biggest problem was that you didn't know whose war you were fighting. Like Peter, you denied your master. Like Peter, you said that you didn't know the commander.

You felt ashamed and played into enemy hands. You trusted your own energy and resources, and ended up disgraced and despised. All this left you in bad shape with internal and external pain, virtually incarcerated in a mental prison. The more you concentrate on your seemingly hopeless state, the more the conditions deteriorate. Consequently, you suffer self-denial, and your end looks eminent. Many are the wounds you get when you turn God's battle into a personal encounter!

As we saw from the beginning, when you are in that state, nobody understands what you are actually going through. Unlike among soldiers, no medic department is in sight, and recovery becomes a dream that is fading. As all these happen, all you thought to be your friends or fellow ministers are the very ones who want to crucify you or bury you alive. This deepens your wounds and increases your pain. And that time, the only service they have for you is to make a board meeting with pastors and elders to talk about you and how they have to stop you from getting involved in anything as far the ministry is concerned. In this type of meeting, everything you did, the bad and the good, come out. It is like a burial meeting!

YOUR WOUNDS ARE, TO SATAN, VERY MPORTANT RESOURCES:

When you are in pain, the devil secretly brings more confusing temptations, putting negative information, false accusation, and blaming and criticism in the ears of your heart. The devil will keep telling you that God is no longer on your side and that God actually hates you. In addition, the devil shows you how much people hate you and tries to convince you that God doesn't need you anymore. In those hard times, you lose focus of what you were called to do; you lose the sight of your goal, and your faith and confidence fly away.

When you are thus wounded, you become weak, and it is at this time the devil uses his weapons to distract you from the love of God. You continue to hear more loud negative voices as the devil accuses you, telling you that all people have left you and showing you that everybody hates you. Because of the criticism and mocking from fellow workers, the devil gains ground and uses all the negative words and curses from their mouths to worsen your condition. Those words divert you from what you are supposed to be and turn you into what they say you are. Their words transform you, and you become what they want you to be, and that justifies their judgment. Remember, Judas was given money by the Pharisees to betray Jesus, but after the arrest of Jesus, he took back the money to the Pharisees, who refused the money saying that the money had blood on it as they hypocritically wanted all blame to go to Judas. It was their money, but it had finished the job. They didn't want it because they wanted to remain righteous in their judgments. In the same way, those who betrayed you make sure they finish you, and they remain in their seat of self-righteousness.

³ "When Judas, who had betrayed him, saw that Jesus was condemned, he was seized with remorse and returned the thirty pieces of silver to the chief priests and the elders. ⁴ 'I have sinned,' he said, 'for I have betrayed innocent blood.'
'What is that to us?' they replied. 'That's your responsibility.'
⁵ So Judas threw the money into the temple and left. Then he went away and hanged himself.
⁶ The chief priests picked up the coins and said, 'It is against the law to put this into the treasury, since it is blood money.' ⁷ So they decided to use the money to buy the potter's field as a burial place for foreigners.
⁸ That is why it has been called the Field of Blood to this day."
Matthew 27:3-8

When everybody turns against you, sometimes it becomes necessary to try and fight back to prove that you were right and innocent, but here, the more you want to fight back, the more you become distressed. You start by distrusting everybody, and anger accumulates in your heart against those who betrayed you - your false friends who disappointed you and all who worked together for your downfall. Incidentally, that also increases pain and becomes an ever-increasing burden on your weak shoulders and incessant headache and heartache.

All these turn you into a different person from the person God intended you to be. Alas, from a focused purposeful soldier to a planless civilian! Because of the shame and disgrace, you are no longer able to see yourself the way God sees you. Instead, you see yourself as people that betrayed you portray you.

From all that attacks the devil brings in the spirit of intimidation to cover up your mind and make you feel depressed and oppressed, you find out that you can't pray for yourself, and there is nobody remain on your side to stand with you when you badly need them. Then you start asking yourself why you should do well when everybody pays you back evil. You get more confused and discouraged.

It is like a planned hijack. When one is hijacked, somebody covers his face and eyes so that he can't see what is going on or where they are taking him. They gag his mouth so that he cannot shout for help. The devil acts exactly the same way so that you cannot see where you are going and you can't pray or speak to anybody because everyone has turned away from you.

That is what the bible talked about in the book of Isaiah 53:6 regarding people in this kind of situation.

⁶ "We all, like sheep, have gone astray,
each of us has turned to our own way;
and the Lord has laid on him the iniquity of us all.
⁷ He was oppressed and afflicted, yet he did not open his mouth; he was led like a lamb to the slaughter, and as a sheep before its shearers is silent, so he did not open his mouth. ⁸ By oppression and judgment, he was taken away. Yet who of his

generation protested? For he was cut off from the land of the living; for the transgression of my people he was punished."
Isaiah 53:6-9

I have wonderful good news for you today: Thank God, your heavenly Father didn't judge you and blame you the way your friends did. For your friends were like Pharisees to you; they held a power of the law and stones in their hand and were full of the evil spirit of self-righteousness, and they were hell-bent to stone you to death. But Jesus is the one with the final word and holds the power over life and death.

Your friends and colleagues treated you like the teachers and Pharisees who wanted to stone the woman who was caught in adultery, but Jesus treated the woman's case very carefully. After all, she was on the last hour of her death because she was already judged to be killed by stoning. The good news is Jesus has been waiting for you to deal with your case before he comes because you are still his chosen one.

[3] "The teachers of the law and the Pharisees brought in a woman caught in adultery. They made her stand before the group [4] and said to Jesus, 'Teacher, this woman was caught in the act of adultery. [5] In the Law, Moses commanded us to stone such women. Now what do you say?' [6] They were using this question as a trap, in order to have a basis for accusing him. But Jesus bent down and started to write on the ground with his finger. [7] When they kept on questioning him, he straightened up and said to them, 'Let any one of you who is without sin be the first to throw a stone at her.'
John 8:3-7

Their judgment was to stone her to death, but Jesus gave her a second chance to live because he knew that when he would die on the cross, this woman's sins would be forgiven.

My friend, God has not yet done away with you. Let us look at Simon Peter and the disciples. They had a talk with Jesus about what was going to happen, and Jesus told Peter before time that he was going to deny him.

Peter declared,

"Even if I have to die with you, I will never disown you."
Matthew 26:35

And all the other disciples said the same. But you can imagine with all that discussion, Peter still forgot the promise and denied Jesus when he was confronted by some girl?

"Now Peter was sitting out in the courtyard,
and a servant girl came to him.
'You also were with Jesus of Galilee,' she said.
But he denied it before them all.
'I don't know what you're talking about,' he said."

Peter denying Jesus did not mark his end, and Jesus didn't say," Go away Peter, you are no longer my disciple." No, but others said whatever they wanted to say about Peter that day.

You can imagine somebody who was hurt by that kind of blow from the enemy. Like Peter, we look around and see that nobody is ready to take care of our wounds. Think about his pain and shame and about how disgraced Peter had felt at that time. Indeed, Judas was not able to contain the shame. He ignobly hanged himself to a tree and died.

Judas was not able to contain the shame. He ignobly hanged himself to a tree and died 4 Saying, I have sinned in that I have betrayed the innocent blood. And they said, What is that to us? see thou to that.5 And he cast down the pieces of silver in the temple, and departed, and went and hanged himself. Mt 27:4-5

Today, we have thousands of gospel ministers and believers who are down because of the pain from their wounds, and they have nobody to turn to for their restoration. If you are among them, this is your opportunity to focus and raise up arms or end exactly like Judas Iscariot.

Be ready to turn your eyes and ears away from what people say about you and turn your focus to the Lord your God, who has your life in his hands and who has the last word.

For the devil wants to take away the pleasure you have, and he wants to steal all of God's promises and blessings that you have. That is why he attacks you, to distract you from your concentration on God's plan and progress. That is the reason the bible says in Revelation 3:10-11:

[10] "Since you have kept my command to endure patiently, I will also keep you from the hour of trial that is going to come on the whole world
to test the inhabitants of the earth.
[11] I am coming soon. Hold on to what you have, so that no one will take your crown."

The demonic purpose the wound serves is for you to lose your crown, but the good news is that your heavenly Father has not given you up, and he is not yet done with you. Rise up from whatever was holding you down.

(4)

OUR HEAVENLY FATHER WANTS TO ERASE YOUR DISGRACE

As we are about to see in the word of God, the above has always been His plan from the beginning when he gave his only son to die for our sins. He doesn't want to lose any soul after the sacrifice of his son. He still keeps his word as Father, Redeemer, and Savior. That is the reason He wants to remove the disgrace and shame from you, so that he raises you back for you to spiritually live again.

In the book of Joshua, the children of Israel were treated like slaves. Some were born in slavery and died in slavery. They didn't have a single day in their life to taste being free people, and they had no value in the eyes of Egyptians.

They had pain without cure; they were oppressed by Egyptian, and their wounds were so deep in their hearts, seeing children, parents, and grandparents beaten daily and being treated worse than animals, constructing structures whose purpose they didn't know.

Think about what they used to go through in their lives and the pain with the humiliation they were subjected to, living in a foreign land. But one day, as written in the book of Joshua 5:9, the children of Israelites were told that God was going to remove the disgrace of Egypt from you.

Today, I don't know how bad your enemies have treated you, and I don't know how much pain and shame you've gone through, but here, below, I have a piece of good news for you.

> *"Then the Lord said to Joshua,*
> *'Today I have rolled away from the reproach*
> *and disgrace of Egypt from you.'"*
> *Joshua 5:9*

Today is your day, please take these words to rescue yourself. It is God telling you like he told the Israelites in Egypt. He has rolled away the disgrace and the shame imposed on you by your enemies and is taking away the evil curse from your head.

The bible tells us the name of the place where God removed the disgrace from the children of Israel – it is called Gilgal until this day. My friend, whatever you went through, whatever happened to you, this day, you are stepping in your land of Gilgal in your life.

The scripture says,

> *"Then the Lord said to Joshua,*
> *'Today, I have rolled away the reproach of Egypt from you,*
> *so the place has been called Gilgal to this day."*
> *Joshua 5:9*

It is your time to come back and fit yourself into your God's original plan, so that you may walk in your blessings, and God receives his glory through your life.

THE ATTACK AND ROOTS OF DISGRACE:

The evil attacks and betrayals, in most cases, come from the agent of Satan, the devil. But on most of occasions, Satan uses those you call your friends, your relatives, and those who are close to you to fulfill his demonic plans. These always tend to know you in and out even more than you know yourself.

As it was written, the enemy will work in those we think are on our side; they may be our neighbors, and some will be our siblings or even co-workers. Therefore, my friend, don't be surprised when this happens because it is written in the bible:

> *^{34} "Do not suppose that I have come to bring peace to the earth. I did not come to bring peace, but a sword.*
> *^{35} For I have come to turn*
> *a man against his father, a daughter against her mother, a daughter-in-law against her mother-in-law — ^{36} a man's enemies will be the members of his own household."*
> *Matthew 10:34-36*

Always, when the devil comes in with temptations, things which are not supposed to happen to you start to happen. That is when devil tries to divert you from God's planned course. The devil's plan is to take your focus from God. The devil raises dusts of disappointment and disgrace, and you become blind to divine realties. The devil assembles a team, including the jealous and covetous people around you and those always pushed by spirit competition. Some are very proud, while others are too selfish to think about anybody else.

Remember, Jesus was betrayed by Judas Iscariot, one of his close disciples who was trusted with the finances of the whole team of twelve disciples and their master. Judas knew about the resources of the team. Being the financial manager who kept the money purse means he was close in Jesus' ministry.

The hypocritical Pharisees looked into many different ways to catch and kill Jesus. They tried many times by setting traps for him, but all they tried was not working until they got Judas, who was a money-loving thief, to fulfill the prophecy as Jesus' disciple. The Pharisees knew how close he was to Jesus.

> *3 "When Judas, who had betrayed him,*
> *saw that Jesus was condemned,*
> *he was seized with remorse and returned the thirty pieces of silver to the chief priests and the elders.*
> *4 'I have sinned,' he said, 'for I have betrayed innocent blood.'*
> *'What is that to us?' they replied. 'That's your responsibility.'*
> *5 So Judas threw the money into the temple and left.*
> *Then he went away and hanged himself."*
> *Mt. 27:3-5*

The Philistines tried all ways they could to kill Samson without success. When Samson's enemies failed to defeat him, they let him a have a beautiful friend. Alas, they didn't give him someone to fight, but a friend called Delilah to dupe him into complacency.

[15] "Then she said to him, 'How can you say, I love you, when you won't confide in me? This is the third time you have made a fool of me and haven't told me the secret of your great strength.' [16] With

such nagging she prodded him day after day until he was sick to death of it.

¹⁷ So he told her everything. 'No razor has ever been used on my head,' he said,

'because I have been a Nazirite dedicated to God from my mother's womb.

If my head were shaved, my strength would leave me, and I would become as weak as any other man.'

¹⁸ When Delilah saw that he had told her everything, she sent word to the rulers of the Philistines, 'Come back once more; he has told me everything.'

So the rulers of the Philistines returned with the silver in their hands. ¹⁹ After putting him to sleep on her lap, she called for someone to shave off the seven braids of his hair, and so began to subdue him.

And his strength left him.
²⁰ Then she called, 'Samson, the Philistines are upon you!'
He awoke from his sleep and thought, 'I'll go out as before and shake myself free.' But he did not know that the Lord had left him.
²¹ Then the Philistines seized him, gouged out his eyes and took him down to Gaza.
Binding him with bronze shackles,
they set him to grinding grain in the prison."
Judges 16:15-21

Delilah was showing Samson how much she loved him as she planned the betrayal. Even in our day today, we meet with such kinds of love pretenders and fall into their traps. Because Samson responded to her, his love cost him his life. Like Pharisees, the Philistines knew that the worst enemy is always the one close to you. Like Judas was to Jesus, Delilah was very close to Samson, and your fellow ministers, co-workers, and fellow believers are never far from you.

We don't say that we should not have friends or relatives, but the truth is that the most efficient way the devil is using to destroy our ministries is using fellow ministers.

Let us take the example of Joseph in the book of Genesis. The bible tells us that when Joseph had a dream, his brothers hated him more. That means that before Joseph's dream, his brothers hated him. Apart from being loved by his father, Jacob, who also loved them, there was no clear reason of hating him. The bible tells us that after the dream, they hated him more.

"Joseph had a dream, and when he told it to his brothers, they hated him all the more.
He said to them, 'Listen to this dream I had:
We were binding sheaves of grain out in the field when suddenly, my sheaf rose and stood upright, while your sheaves gathered around mine and bowed down to it.'"
Gen 37:5-6

Joseph's dream wasn't bad for Joseph, but he was hated for it. Therefore, people can hate you for no good or bad reason. Joseph thought he was sharing a dream with his father and his brothers, but this dream almost cost him his life. Sometimes, you get a blessing, and it becomes a problem to someone else. Sometimes, the situation becomes so bad that escaping the problems becomes impossible, hence the bruises and wounds.

Remember, as I told you for the disgracing and disappointing attacks, the devil uses the closest people around you. Joseph's problem arose within the family; no stranger was involved in this problem. These are his real brothers. If you can remember, those who worked hard for your downfall are your close friends; maybe some are even relatives. Some were helped by you to rise to their present positions in ministry.

They start nicknaming, and you don't know what they call you while you are away. That is what they did to Joseph when they gave him the name of "the dreamer." His brothers did all this evil because of jealousy and disgraced him, and when they threw him into the pit in the desert, they wanted him to die. That is the reason for this book - to dress up your wound so that you don't die in the pit where your friends have dumped you.

Can we imagine what was in Joseph's heart about his brothers when he was still in that pit? He had the pain of physical bruises and wounds inside his heart. Indeed, these internal wounds are more painful and certainly take longer to heal. When our Lord Jesus' pain was at its maximum point, it was the internal that hurt him most. He talked about the pain in his soul.

> *"He took Peter and the two sons of Zebedee along with him, and he began to be sorrowful and troubled.*
> *Then he said to them, 'My soul is overwhelmed with sorrow to the point of death. Stay here and keep watch with me.'"*
> *Mt. 26:37-38*

Have you ever imagined a situation when it is not just your body suffering, but also your soul?

Do you remember when they made up a fake and embarrassing story about you or your colleague? When they betrayed you, they said they had the evidence to prove you guilty. Because it is the devil supporting those who accuse you, he always provides them the physical evidence to make sure you are convicted. He ensures that no one remains on your side, and very few will believe your words anymore because the evidence weaved by the devil looks water-tight, at least in the eyes of men. When everybody turns his or her back against you, at that moment, you take in the spirit of rejection.

THE DEVIL'S EVIDENCE:

As we all know happens in the courtroom, the judge always wants the proof to convict the suspect of the crime, and he can judge him or her according to the proof brought to court. Let me tell you, the devil knows this, and he knows how to produce the proof.

In the book of Genesis, we see Joseph's brothers creating factual evidence to take to their father as proof of the death of his son. They took Joseph's robe, slaughtered a goat, and dipped Joseph's robe in the blood so that when they went back home to Jacob, they had evidence of Joseph's death. When he saw Joseph's robe full of blood, he believed that his son was dead. Jacob believed all the lies from his sons' story that Joseph had been killed by wild animal.

"Then they got Joseph's robe, slaughtered a goat, and dipped the robe in the blood. They took the ornate robe back to their father and said, 'We found this. Examine it to see whether it is your son's robe.' He recognized it and said, 'It is my son's robe! Some ferocious animal has devoured him. Joseph has surely been torn to pieces.' Then Jacob tore his clothes, put on sackcloth, and mourned for his son many days."
Genesis 37:31-33

The Wounded Soldier

Look at this point: when they took the robe to their father, they said, "We found this. Examine it to see whether it is your son's robe." This is what people do to destroy others; they start to examine you and check your integrity above their lies to prove you guilty using their seemingly foolproof evidence, even when it is 100% wrong. In the same way, many believed the lies about you which were forged by your accusers, who were always good at producing fake evidence.

We still find the second evidence about Joseph in the Genesis 39:1-16, when Potiphar's wife falsely accuses Joseph. When Potiphar's wife desires to sleep with Joseph, and Joseph refuses to go to bed with her, she falsely accused Joseph, and to make crime true and the evidence strong, she had proof to show her husband to prove that Joseph was the worst servant in the house.

It is for this reason that when Potiphar came back, his wife was waiting with a piece of cloth from Joseph's cloak in her hands as evidence. The devil's evidence against innocent men of God is always available. After Potiphar saw the evidence from his wife, Joseph's life was doomed, and his fate was sealed. He had nothing to say, and nobody wanted to reason to him.

Notably, Joseph had been taken down to Egypt. Potiphar, an Egyptian who was one of Pharaoh's officials, the captain of the guard, bought him from the Ishmaelites who had brought him to Egypt for sale.

As usual, the Lord was with Joseph so that he prospered, and he lived in the house of his Egyptian master. When his master saw that the Lord was with him and that the Lord gave him success in everything he did, Joseph found favor in his eyes and became his attendant. Potiphar put him in charge of his household, and he entrusted to his care everything he owned. From the time he put him in charge of his household and all that he owned, the Lord blessed the household of the Egyptian because of Joseph. The blessing of the Lord was on everything Potiphar had, both in the house and in the field, so Potiphar left everything he had in Joseph's care; with Joseph in charge, he did not concern himself with anything except the food he ate. What a wonderful servant! Trouble would come from unexpected angle.

> *"Now Joseph was well-built and handsome,*
> *and after a while, his master's wife took notice of Joseph and said,*
> *'Come to bed with me!'*
>
> *But he refused. 'With me in charge,' he told her, 'my master does not concern himself with anything in the house; everything he owns he has entrusted to my care.*
>
> *No one is greater in this house than I am. My master has withheld nothing from me except you because you are his wife. How then could I do such a wicked thing and sin against God?'*
>
> *And though she spoke to Joseph day after day, he refused to go to bed with her or even be with her.*
>
> *One day, he went into the house to attend to his duties, and none of the household servants was inside.*
>
> *She caught him by his cloak and said, 'Come to bed with me!' But he left his cloak in her hand and ran out of the house.*
>
> *When she saw that he had left his cloak in her hand and had run out of the house,*
>
> *she called her household servants. 'Look,' she said to them, 'this Hebrew has been brought to us to make sport of us! He came in here to sleep with me, but I screamed.*
>
> *When he heard me scream for help, he left his cloak beside me and ran out of the house.'*
>
> *She kept his cloak beside her until his master came home."*
> ***Genesis 39:7-16***

Note these points: these are different pieces of evidence in different cases, taking place in different places to one person. Even with all this evidence, nothing stopped Joseph from catching up with is destiny. He didn't shy away because of the shame caused by Potiphar's wife; the truth was in his heart, and inside, he was upright and strong. The God of his fathers was fully awake!

I don't know your accusers or how many pieces of evidence they have before this worldly court. When the devil uses people to destroy others or work on their downfall, he will avail evidence to pin down their victims. It doesn't matter whether it is true or false. They will have evidence and mark you with the devil, and the truth and the public perception may be poles apart! My friend, I don't know how much you have gone through or how hard it has been. Maybe you too went to prison, like Joseph. Some have even died, but what cannot and shall not die is the truth.

God has not given up with you. God didn't give up on Joseph, and Jesus didn't give up with Peter for denying him. God still counts on you; that is the reason why you still live to tell the story.

God is going to remove the disgrace, shame, and reproach tagged on you by your enemies. He is going to take away the burden they put on you and set you permanently free, regardless of the evidence which was brought to prove your guilty. Your God, the Lord, is going to remove and heal all the wounds from the devil and erase all the stories they made up. He is taking away all conflicts brought forward by your jealous co-workers because of empty competition. He will chastise those who told lies about you and those jealous because of your progress. Thank God your Lord knows the truth and is compassionate, and nothing is hidden from Him.

My friend, as the reading cleans you, please work hand in hand with the doctor to take the medicine as directed, and the healing is yours. The Lord God knows you very well, actually better than you think. He does not only understand your situation; He is above all a kind and extremely loving father. It is an obligation for you to say;

> *"Therefore do not be like them.*
> *For your Father knows the things you*
> *have need of before you ask Him.*
> *9 In this manner,*
> *therefore, pray:*
> *Our Father in heaven,*
> *Hallowed be Your name.*
> *10 Your kingdom come.*
> *Your will be done*
> *On earth as it is in heaven.*
> *11 Give us this day our daily bread.*
> *12 And forgive us our debts,*
> *As we forgive our debtors.*
> *13 And do not lead us into temptation,*
> *But deliver us from the evil one.*
> *For Yours is the kingdom and the power*
> *and the glory forever. Amen.*
> *Mt. 6:8-13*

(5)

YOU MATTER IN THE EYES OF YOUR HEAVENLY FATHER

Let us start with the root cause of your rejection, the source of disgrace and disappointment. We found out it always starts with the close friends and people around you, your relatives and fellow ministers.

As we saw with Joseph, it was his real brothers who rejected him, hated him, and worked on his downfall. Let us now dwell on your problem and the way you got wounded. If you can remember well, it started with those you thought to be friends at your place of work or in your ministry.

These people who rose against you started a battle with their hearts, and their fight is based on what you don't know or knew little about. Nevertheless, the devil had already started the battle within their hearts, and they used to smile and laugh with you, but they had a war going on within their hearts. From that time while the battle went on inside them, they started speaking negatively about you when you were away. But when you are around, everything is fine, good, and peaceful.

For the example, let us use the name Brother Tom as a minister of gospel; these people who are working for brother Tom's downfall tell their friend while talking about Brother Tom, "We know him very well. He calls himself a minister but is full of lies, and we doubt his character." When someone tries to ask them how much they know about and how long they have known Tom, they will simply say they know him, even his background from his hometown, and they will say he is from a very poor family, didn't finish his education, is a dropout guy, and used to feed himself on the church food and sometimes used drugs, and many more negative evil words.

The only history and information they have about Tom is all negative, yet there is positive news about Tom which they don't want to say. Therefore, with all the negative news about Tom, they try to prove to people that they know him in and out, as they normally say. They make sure people believe their lies at all costs. And all these who hear the negative news about you start seeing you differently with a different perspective and a different judgment. They start to change their attitude towards you. Your enemies rejoice because they are slowly but surely destroying you. They nickname you and give you names behind your back. By the time you get to know a lot of damage has been done, it is too late to heal the wound.

Please note this: with all the lies spread about you by those who claim to know you, the truth is not one of them knows you; they don't know who you are, and they have no idea at all who you are. Yes, they know the little they see with their naked eyes, but they don't know anything about the spirit deep inside you. There is the big and important part of you they know not. That is the real you that matters in the eyes of God, your maker.

They don't know anything which is on God's heart about you. Whatever they said and the way they treated you was based on human understanding, and they did it with the canal mind or tunnel vision. Unfortunately, you too took them seriously because you thought that everything they did to you, they were doing in the name of God. The bible tells us in the book of Isaiah that people will be in meetings, talking and judging others in the name of serving God.

"Behold, they shall surely gather together, but not by me: whosoever shall gather together against thee shall fall for thy sake if anyone does attack you."
Isaiah 54:15

As we continue to dress up your wounds, I would like you to see yourself the way God sees you. They are the main facts we are going to see, which will help you to change your attitude about yourself to see a better mirror image of your personality.

Because of what you have been going through or what happened to you, the devil tried to use that situation to change your focus from God's original plan about you to what people say about you. When you heard the accusers all blaming you from left to right, from north to south, from every side, that is when you got distracted and dropped down your trust from God and took the words that came into your ears and what you saw with your naked eyes as gospel truth. You were bombarded with negative and evil words, and your wounds spread down to your heart, your mind, and even your soul. Then the devil enjoyed this and raised the temperatures of the shame and fear in your life, which led you into isolation.

As we earlier said, not one of those people that are authors of your tragedy knows you. However, it becomes worse if all these things happen to you when you don't know and understand yourself because if all your enemies don't know and understand you, at least you must know who you are in Christ. We are going to see examples of people who went through more than what you can imagine, but who knew who they were and knew themselves from inside their hearts.

Let us come face to face with some facts about who we are in relation with our God. When God called you to serve Him, none of your friends was called to meet Him to decide what you were going to do. God didn't ask for their approval about whether you are fit to serve or not. They don't know why God picked you for his ministry. They don't have any idea what was on God's heart about you; that is the reason we need to work from inside, so as to see yourself the way God sees you. This is imperative because it is personal relationship between you and God.

When God looks down to look at you, what does he see? He wants to see your true and original form, not a duplicate other people have produced to drive you away from the right course. God wants to see you enjoying all his blessings and honoring Him.

The main problem in human nature is that people want human approval above God's endorsement. We want people to be our fans, and we want many people to accept us. When they don't do so, we start to think of ourselves as failures. When people reject, it doesn't mean God has disowned you.

My friend, take this point seriously. Even if the whole world forsakes, when God approves you, all is well and you are homeward bound. Focus on His word; you don't need human approval. And all these brethren remember, each of them has his own cross has to carry. Forget about them and carry your cross and follow Christ and go forward. The bible says:

"Then he said to them all: 'Whoever wants to be my disciple must deny themselves and take up their cross daily and follow me. For whoever wants to save their life will lose it, but whoever loses their life for me will save it.'"
Lk. 9:23-24

Remember when you deeply felt pain of rejection and cried of tiredness and shame behind closed doors, where you didn't want anybody to see you or to know that you are crying; at that time, God was there with you, watching you, waiting for you to come down and fall to your knees before Him, for He alone has the healing balm of Gilead, and you will be covered by his grace. You will be alive, not because people want you to be, but as your God said as long as He lives, you too shall live. You are progressing not because people want you to progress. You need to know that anything you have is by the grace of your heavenly Father. He paid the ransom to set you free when He prayed with pain in Gethsemane.

"Then he said to them, 'My soul is overwhelmed with sorrow to the point of death. Stay here and keep watch with me.' Going a little farther, he fell with his face to the ground and prayed, 'My Father, if it is possible, may this cup be taken from me. Yet not as I will, but as you will.'"

Our Lord Jesus was praying and crying the whole night just for your survival. I don't know how many times you hid behind the closet and went through tears alone and didn't want people to see you or know that you were crying. Remember, Jesus sweated blood from the mental anguish so that you could be set free.

> *"And being in anguish, he prayed more earnestly, and his sweat was like drops of blood falling to the ground."*
> *"Luke 22:44"*

His disciples, poor men, could not understand what their master was going through. That is one of the reasons they were asleep most of the time when Jesus went to check and wake them up. They were able to know only what they saw with their eyes. The world has not changed much since then. Jesus wakes them up, but they go back into slumber.

Think about it. Jesus is praying and in great pain, as the bible tells us, because one of his disciples is the one who betrayed him, and those still with him were sleeping, unable to persist for even one hour. That is also another deep pain you can imagine but have not yet gone through. When you start feeling that your God has left you, that is the mother of all pains.

> [40] *"Then he returned to his disciples and found them sleeping. 'Couldn't you men keep watch with me for one hour?' he asked Peter.*
> [41] *'Watch and pray so that you will not fall into temptation.* **The spirit is willing,** *but the flesh is weak.'*
> [42] *He went away a second time and prayed, 'My Father, if it is not possible for this cup to be taken away unless I drink it, may your will be done.'*
> [43] *When he came back, he again found them sleeping, because their eyes were heavy.*

*⁴⁴ So he left them and went away once more and prayed the third time,
saying the same thing. ⁴⁵ Then he returned to the disciples and said to them, 'Are you still sleeping and resting? Look, the hour has come, and the Son of Man is delivered into the hands of sinners. ⁴⁶ Rise! Let us go! Here comes my betrayer.'"
Mt. 26:40-46*

As you went through your battle and cried in the secret place, you realized that you remain alone. During that hard time, maybe you felt that your God had left you. You were so discouraged, stopped crying and fighting, and decided to keep quiet. Maybe you didn't want to continue with the fight. That happens to many different people. Because every arrow from the enemy was coming towards you, and you couldn't fight back, you turned away and felt like running away from the people because you didn't see any solution. And your enemies were happy; they thought you were finished.

But let us look at what Job went through: In the book of Job, chapter 2, we learn some good lessons from Job, He was a man of God like you. He was loved by God, yet all these problems happened in his life. There is nowhere it is written that Job did anything wrong or sinned, but:

*"Then the Lord said to Satan,
'Have you considered my servant Job?
There is no one on earth like him; he is blameless and upright, a man who fears God and shuns evil. And he still maintains his integrity, though you incited me against him to ruin him without any reason.'"*

Regardless of Job's life being blameless and upright, it didn't stop all these calamities from befalling him. You know what happened to you and what you went through, but I don't think it was worse than what Job went through.

Remember, with Job, the devil went to ask permission from God, and from what we read from this story, the devil knows well how faithful you are to your God. And again, what we learn from Job is that He knew who he was in terms of his relationship with his God.

But Job went through a situation which you can only overcome if you know well your relationship with your God. Job faced all the shame and criticisms we go through, and many judged him when he lost everything while others, including his wife, mocked him, saying that he had always called himself a man of God. The bible tells us that everybody turned away from him. I know you too lost friends, but Job lost everybody including wealth and even his children.

Because he had lost everything and everybody, he lay in ashes naked, groaning day and night. When you try to put yourself in his shoes, I think you have a reason to rise up again. We know some face a hard time because of their sin, but Job had not sinned against his God yet is going through a hard time. That is why we should not just judge somebody from what we see, because we don't know why and we don't understand God's heart about the situation.

To compound the tragedy after Job had lost everything, the devil asked God to touch on his body:

"Skin for skin!' Satan replied.
'A man will give all he has for his own life.
But now stretch out your hand and strike his flesh and bones, and
he will surely curse you to your face.'
The Lord said to Satan, 'Very well, then,
he is in your hands; but you must spare his life.'

The Wounded Soldier

So Satan went out from the presence of the Lord and afflicted Job with painful sores from the soles of his feet to the crown of his head."
Job 2:4-7

The bible tells us that Satan wanted one thing: to prove to God that Job can be distracted with all pain and deny or curse his God.

In verse 9, when it becomes worse, it was too bad for Job, but the devil was still losing the battle, and he decided to use Job's wife remaining near him - remember that we saw that the devil will use those around you. Now Job's wife is giving Job advice of destruction to curse God and die!

"Then Job took a piece of broken pottery and scraped himself with it as he sat among the ashes. His wife said to him, 'Are you still maintaining your integrity? Curse God and die.'"

You can imagine Job's situation when his wife tells him to curse his God. That was like a six-inch stab straight into Job's head. I think Job asks himself, if he had to die, why he would need to curse God? But remember why Job's wife asked Job to curse God and die - Satan wanted to prove to God that at a certain level, Job could deny him or curse his God. Job's wife was now being used by the devil so that he could achieve his goal of Job cursing his God. So whatever the evil your friends are doing all the way, they are helping the devil so that you can curse your God and die. The devil knows that you can't curse God and live.

Remarkably, Job had no one remaining on his side, no one to understand what he was going through, no one to comfort him, and no one to try to dress his internal and external wounds, but he survived because he was still focused and still trusting his God. For this reason, he forgets all that people said about him and all the lies about him, and he held strongly on his God, and indeed, his plan did not let him down. What was written in the scriptures, in the book of Matthew, comes to pass where it is said that one's enemies will be from his own household, as we see in Job's life.

In time, we became the original piece God made. As you know, God doesn't make counterfeits. He creates originals. Always remember you are his unique creation. When you go through difficulties and go on praying and crying, it changes the way you used to think about yourself. You start to get a different attitude about people and about yourself. The original, which changed when you were wounded, comes back, allowing God to effect the plans he had upon your creation.

Therefore, it is time to come back to God's original plan as his beloved sons and daughters and start looking at yourself the way God beholds you in his grand plan. Let us endeavor to find out who we are in face of our heavenly Father. Therefore, at this time, we should not give time or attention to negative words from creatures when the creator is with us. The bible says;

"Never will I leave you; never will I forsake you.'
⁶ So we say with confidence,
'The Lord is my helper; I will not be afraid. What can mere mortals do to me?"'
Hebrews 13:5-6

As a living example, we look at David, son of Jesse, and what happened to him when he went to visit and take some food to his brother on the battlefront. When David heard how Goliath abused and blasphemed the name of the Lord, he was uncomfortable and wanted to do something about it, but since he was not a soldier, everybody despised him as a mere shepherd boy supposed to be looking after sheep. Sadly, his real elder brother, Eliab, for whom he had brought provisions, led those who scolded him. He even called him wicked. David knew that all people who despised him, including his brother, did not understand who he was. David was seeing himself in the picture of his God. He believed in his God, and that is why he didn't care whatever these people were saying bad things of him. They later discovered that their victory was in David who acted as guided by his God.

Now back to our point, whatever was said or whatever they thought about you, these people have no idea who are you to your God. They don't know God's plans for you. Therefore, don't give any value to their negative words. Don't let your heart entertain these evil words from their mouth.

(6)

THE DIVINE ANTIDOTE:

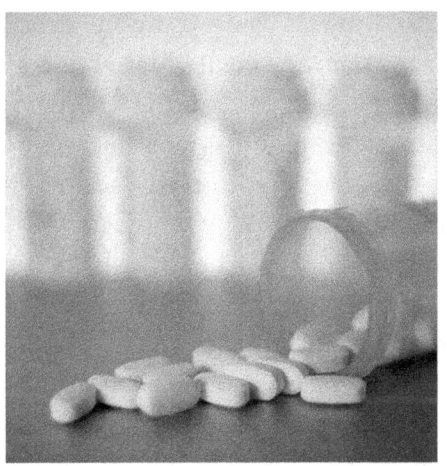

As it is in God's plan to remove the reproach the enemy has heaped upon you, He is going to heal you from your wounds, both on the body and in the soul. Remember, you are not alone; Jesus Christ our Lord was betrayed by his disciple and close friend when He was on frontline serving his heavenly Father.

When we go to the hospital to meet a doctor, since they are different types of sickness and different types of sick people, all doctors ask you questions about how you are feeling and which part of your body pains you and for how long. They do this because you are the one who knows what hurts your body. Notably, the doctor starts to treat you on the basis of the information you give him, and therefore, you play a fundamental role in your own treatment.

When a doctor discovers what you are suffering from, he gives a medicine according to your sickness for your cure. That is the same thing that happens in soldier's sickbays or hospitals. And it is your responsibility as the sick person to work hand in hand with doctor and use the medicine as per the doctor's description.

Back to our point, it is you who knows what happened to you, the way you felt when you were attacked, and your inner feelings when they created falsehood about you and betrayed you. In short, you are the one who understands best the pain, shame, and disgrace you went through.

Therefore, we are going to try to address your problem based on the truth inside your heart. When you face the truth from inside your heart, it helps to bring quick recovery because you don't need a doctor to guess or do many different checks to get to the problem. Therefore, on this type of problem, you know without asking anybody a question. But if you are still confused, you can pray the prayer of David, because when David was not sure of his stand with the Lord, he prayed for the Lord to search his heart.

> [23] *"Search me, God, and know my heart; test me and know my anxious thoughts.* [24] *See if there is any offensive way in me, and lead me in the way everlasting."*
> *Psalms 139:23-24*

David was a king, but knew how to keep his relationship with God. In being a king, there was a temptation of everybody talking positive about you and people praising you. It is easy to feel loved and powerful and forget who you are with your God. King David, however, knew that he could not hide his heart away because God knows all about you, even the things you forgot or those don't even know. He knows all about you.

Therefore, treatment will be based on the real truth within your heart, and that truth is known by you. It is your responsibility to face that truth within you. To achieve this, you have to forget what people said about you or what they think about you. Then, we are all going to see the way God sees you and see the truth within your heart. When you face both your truth and your God, that will be the turning point of your life. That is so because when God looks down at you, He sees only the truth about you: the true picture of his creation.

Therefore, from the truth you have in you, the good news is that your God knows the same truth in your heart. So whether they you say you sinned against your God or you didn't do anything right, it doesn't matter!! With or without sin, the good news there is your medicine and your healing is at hand. Even though you didn't deserve to be treated, the doctor is not against you. The bible says:

> *"Even though your sins are as red as crimson,*
> *they will be as white as snow."*
> *Isaiah 1:18*

All is therefore built upon your truth. The truth is the medicine for any weakness or sin that took place in your life. Please keep that truth in you, for your healing rotates round that truth. We are going to see what the word of God says about that what happened to you.

Remember, the word of God said according to the book of Revelation, Satan the accuser has many agents who are around us doing work for him by accusing us.

"Then I heard a loud voice in heaven say:
'Now have come the salvation and the power and the kingdom of
our God,
and the authority of his Messiah.
For the accuser of our brothers and sisters,
who accuses them before our God, day and night,
has been hurled down.'"
Rev. 12:10.

This shows the power behind all that have been accusing you. They were under the power your accuser, who is the devil.

After revealing your accuser, the bible tells you what your God says about that - what happens to you if there was something wrong you committed or if anything negative took place. At this stage, you need to forget all that people said and focus on the truth within yourself and the mercy of your God. This is so because your God is not among your accusers, but He is your Lord and personal Savior.

The word of God is very clear in the book of 2 Timothy 3:16-17, where it says that God's word is useful to teach us to realize what is wrong in our lives, corrects us when we are wrong, and teaches the right way; it doesn't accuse us, and its aim is not to crucify us.

It is God's plan that when we go the wrong way, we are corrected because we are his sons and daughters, and God wants his servants to be strong.

"All Scripture is God-breathed and is useful for teaching,
rebuking, correcting and training in righteousness,

so that the servant of God may be thoroughly equipped for every good work"
2 Timothy 3:16

Therefore, we are still dealing with the problem brought by the sin committed by God's servant. Unfortunately, this always happens in our life, but God's grace is abundant. As of the word of God, all have sinned and come short of His glory.

²³ "For all have sinned and fall short of the glory of God, ²⁴ and all are justified freely by his grace through the redemption that came by Christ Jesus.
²⁵ God presented Christ as a sacrifice of atonement, through the shedding of his blood — to be received by faith. He did this to demonstrate his righteousness, because in his forbearance he had left the sins committed beforehand unpunished—
²⁶ he did it to demonstrate his righteousness at the present time, so as to be just and the one who justifies those who have faith in Jesus."
Romans 3:23-26

Therefore, if all of us have sinned, and all of us we were given the opportunity to repent and be forgiven the same way, you have the same grace to come back to your Father and repent on all your sins. There is deep truth about such a situation of being a victim of sin, and the word of God tells us very clearly about such a situation:

The Wounded Soldier

"Brothers and sisters, if someone is caught in a sin,
you who live by the Spirit should restore that person gently.
But watch yourselves, or you also may be tempted.
Carry each other's burdens, and in this way,
you will fulfill the law of Christ."
Gal. 6:1-2

We will talk about gently restoring that person who sinned. By saying these words, He knew that there would be a time his servant would become weak and commit sins. That is the reason He asks us to handle gently these that fall in sin.

Because every doctor has to work gently on the sick person, he comes closer to the patient and with a loving voice, calmly speaks encouraging words to him, touches him gently where he feels pain, and makes sure he doesn't hurt him or her. That means that when our brothers and sisters are in such a situation of pain due to wounds caused by shame or other problems, or by the circumstances beyond their control, we have to be close to them, not run away or turn our backs on them. That situation is when they need us most; there is saying that a friend in need is a friend indeed!

That is the main point our Lord Jesus demonstrated when the Pharisees came to him with the power of the law, with stones in their hands ready to kill the woman who had been caught in sin. Jesus handled the situation gently, as we see in the scriptures:

[3] "The teachers of the law and the Pharisees brought in a woman caught in adultery.
They made her stand before the group [4] and said to Jesus,
'Teacher, this woman was caught in the act of adultery.
[5] In the Law, Moses commanded us to stone such women.

Now what do you say?' ⁶ *They were using this question as a trap, in order to have a basis for accusing him. But Jesus bent down and started to write on the ground with his finger.*
⁷ When they kept on questioning him, he straightened up and said to them, 'Let any one of you who is without sin be the first to throw a stone at her.'"

John 8:3-7 My friend, as you read this book, since we are all sinners, this is your medicine bottle, and the description is written on it for your healing and mine.

Therefore, if you had any sin you know inside your heart, you have to turn to the Lord Jesus because He said in his word:

"Come now, let us settle the matter,' says the Lord. 'Though your sins are like scarlet, they shall be as white as snow; though they are red as crimson, they shall be like wool.'"
Isaiah 1:18

This the word from your God and his plans for you; He does not hate you and has not rejected you, He is still calling you to come forward for repentance.

That is the reason you have to repent your sins now because your Lord Jesus is waiting to wash you from all your sins and restore you in your position as a child of a God. Don't, therefore, miss the opportunity for your healing and restoration. You know how far you have fallen from the grace and salvation, which was freely given to you by your Savior, but like Peter, you too denied and disowned the master, not once, but three times:

> *⁶⁹ "Now Peter was sitting out in the courtyard, and a servant girl came to him. 'You also were with Jesus of Galilee,' she said. ⁷⁰ But he denied it before them all. 'I don't know what you're talking about,' he said. ⁷¹ Then he went out to the gateway, where another servant girl saw him and said to the people there, 'This fellow was with Jesus of Nazareth.'*
> *⁷² He denied it again, with an oath: 'I don't know the man!'*
> *⁷³ After a little while, those standing there went up to Peter and said, 'Surely you are one of them; your accent gives you away.'*
> *⁷⁴ Then he began to call down curses, and he swore to them, 'I don't know the man!' Immediately a rooster crowed."*
> *Mt 26:69-74*

Peter repeatedly denied his Savior but was not rejected. He repented and was restored to his position of Apostle and became the first preacher who preached on the Pentecost, where thousands believed in Jesus Christ that same day.

Now, you don't deserve rejection, and nobody has the power to judge you. You didn't deserve the curses and the disgrace. According to the word of your heavenly Father, and as we've said already your main medicine description, you have to repent on your wrongdoings or your sins. Our heavenly Father was waiting for you to hate sin and wrongdoing and do what is right. Repenting and changing from your sin make you a brand new creature ready to stand again.

David knew repentance and asking God forgiveness because he knew, however weak and wrong he was, God still loved him, and when he faced the truth inside his heart and fixed his eyes to God, he was sure of his recovery.

That is why he said:

"Then I acknowledged my sin to you and did not cover up my iniquity. I said, 'I will confess my transgressions to the LORD.' And you forgave the guilt of my sin. When you repent, it breaks the power of guilty inside your heart."
Palms 32:55

The prodigal Son was guilty, but when he faced the truth inside him and repented to his father, he was forgiven and was saved from all the guilt and became a son at home again. We can see that the prodigal son was restored because of his repentance.

The bible tells us something very important about the prodigal son when it said that the prodigal son came to his senses because he had nobody to sympathize with him, nobody came to him for any advice, and no one was willing to talk to him. But with the help of spirit of God, he was able to come back to his senses, which means he came to understand his sins and mistakes and how far he had fallen away from the love of his father. You too can come back your senses today and turn back to your loving Father.

[11] "There was a man who had two sons. [12] The younger one said to his father, 'Father, give me my share of the estate.' So he divided his property between them.
[13] "Not long after that, the younger son got together all he had, set off for a distant country and there squandered his wealth in wild living. [14] After he had spent everything, there was a severe famine in that whole country, and he began to be in need. [15] So he went and hired himself out to a citizen of that country, who sent him to his fields to feed pigs. [16] He longed to fill his stomach with the pods that the pigs were eating, but no one gave him anything.

17 "When he came to his senses, he said, 'How many of my father's hired servants have food to spare, and here I am starving to death! 18 I will set out and go back to my father and say to him: Father, I have sinned against heaven and against you. 19 I am no longer worthy to be called your son; make me like one of your hired servants.'"
Luke 15:11-19

The gate of Heaven is still open, and the Lord your God awaits with open hands for you to repent and turn away from whatever distracts and takes you away from Him. Don't harden your heart - you have to humble yourself and repent. He says repent, as it written in the scripture:

"My people, who are called by my name, will humble themselves and pray and seek my face and turn from their wicked ways, then I will hear from heaven, and I will forgive their sin and will heal their land."
2Chr 7:14

The word of God says in the bible:
23 "The Lord makes firm the steps of the one who delights in him; 24 though he may stumble, he will not fall, for the Lord upholds him with his hand."
Psalms 37:23-24

In Psalms, David talks about how we sometimes get overwhelmed by our sins and what happens through our life, but still our God is ready, waiting to forgive us if we repent. He says in Psalms 65:33 that when we were overwhelmed by sins, he forgave our transgressions. This is your time to seek God's face and speak these words as King David did:

⁸ "My heart says of you, 'Seek his face! Your face, Lord, I will seek. ⁹ Do not hide your face from me, do not turn your servant away in anger; you have been my helper. Do not reject me or forsake me, God my Savior. ¹⁰ Though my father and mother forsake me, the Lord will receive me. ¹¹ Teach me your way, Lord; lead me in a straight path because of my oppressors. ¹² Do not turn me over to the desire of my foes, **for false witnesses rise up against me,** *spouting malicious accusations. ¹³ I remain confident of this: I will see the goodness of the Lord in the land of the living. ¹⁴ Wait for the Lord; be strong and take heart and wait for the Lord."*
Psalms 86:8-14

"You, Lord, are forgiving and good, abounding in love to all who call to you. "Have mercy on me, LORD; heal me, for I have sinned against you."
Psalms 41:44

From generation to generation, God is welcoming those who come to him. He said that he will not turn his face from you, and this is the time you are back, and He is welcoming you. He forgives and forgets.

"If you return to the Lord, then your fellow Israelites and your children will be shown compassion by their captors and will return to this land, for the Lord your God is gracious and compassionate. He will not turn his face from you if you return to him."
2 Ch. 30:9

There are many people who were good believers, but they crashed within the church, and when got wounded, they got out with those wounds and gave up. When they left, they didn't come back to the Church, and that is what the devil wanted - to distract them from the love of God. The big problem is that most people do not realize that the enemy is using them to destroy the body of Christ.

To those who were wounded and say they are innocent and didn't do anything bad to anybody or sin towards God, and those who tried to do their best to help people and serve God faithfully when those thought to be of good help turned against them, now this is for you. Please, this is your time for your healing and revival back to the original plan of God. You are in a good position because the word of God accepts the suffering for good as it says:

"But how is it to your credit if you receive a beating
for doing wrong and endure it?
But if you suffer for doing good and you endure it,
this is commendable before God."
1 Peter 2:20

Now, as we saw in our first treatment of the sinner, it is the same way we shall start to deal with your case. We start by asking you to face the truth which is hidden inside your heart, to face the truth of what exactly happened that led you to get all these painful wounds of shame and disgrace. Don't fight with people to convince them how innocent you are because your God knows the truth.

About your healing, the encouraging words are from the book of Philippians, telling us that it was granted to us on behalf of Christ believing in him and suffering for him.

> *²⁹ "For it has been granted to you on behalf of Christ not only to believe in him, but also to suffer for him, ³⁰ since you are going through the same struggle you saw I had, and now hear that I still have."*
> *Phil 1:29-30*

Therefore, when you face the truth in your heart, take your eyes away from people, and focus them on God because he is the only one who sees the truth you know from your heart. I always tell my friends that you cannot hide away from the truth inside your heart.

Now you are telling us that you used to serve God, and you are innocent, but people within your family or your ministry betrayed you. They accused you, and they did all to make sure that you are destroyed. You worked hard to help most of them to raise in ministry, but they worked toward your downfall.

We understand, and we are very sorry for what you went through, and we are very sorry that nobody understands exactly what happened to you as you were suffering the wounds of shame, curses, negative judgment, and all disgrace on your life until you gave up. But thanks to God, today, you are still alive physically. A God who kept you alive until this day must have a plan for your restoration before He comes back.

This is what is going to happen to restore your anointing he gave you and recover all that the devil took away. He is glorified in name through your life, and that is the God who keeps his word. There were very many ministers who died in pain from their wound, and until today, nobody knows what happened about the anointed minister ending up in vain.

As we said, the sick person works with the doctor and takes his medicine as doctors describe it. Let us start with whatever you went through; my friend, you have to understand you are not alone. Many good ministers of the gospel went through these battles, and most of them were strong and gifted and didn't do anything wrong, but the main problem was the people around them who were supposed to come to their rescue but were the very people who ensnared them and made their failure in just a matter of time.

You kept asking God Why He could not fight for you when He knew well that you were innocent. That is exactly what Job went through. However, good Job and even God gave testimony, but this didn't exonerate him from the torture he went through.

> *"Then the Lord said to Satan,*
> *'Have you considered my servant Job? There is no one on earth like him; he is blameless and upright, a man who fears God and shuns evil. And he still maintains his integrity, though you incited me against him to ruin him without any reason.'"*
> *Job 2:3*

Ultimately, however, God will restore your life because He understands what happened to you, for it started with His son Jesus Christ. Although Jesus was judged and found guilty at every stage, all knew he had not sinned. Even then, he was beaten and stripped naked, and his clothes were shared among the tormentors. Therefore, friend, whether or not the devil will still try to destroy you, you are safer in Christ Jesus, and that is the reason you should not give up

> [13] *"But rejoice in as much as you participate in the sufferings of Christ, so that you may be overjoyed when his glory is revealed.*

¹⁴ If you are insulted because of the name of Christ, you are blessed, for the Spirit of glory and of God rests on you.
¹⁵ If you suffer, it should not be as a murderer or thief or any other kind of criminal, or even as a meddler.
¹⁶ However, if you suffer as a Christian, do not be ashamed, but praise God that you bear that name.
¹⁷ For it is time for judgment to begin with God's household; and if it begins with us, what will the outcome be for those who do not obey the gospel of God?"
1 Peter 4:13-17

+ This shows us that whatever we are going through, good or bad, our God is with us and knows everything about us.

The word of God is very clear about how much God shows his compassion to you.

"For he will deliver the needy who cry out, the afflicted who have no one to help. He will take pity on the weak and the needy and save the needy from death. He will rescue them from oppression and violence, for precious is their blood in his sight."
Psalms 72:12-14

The good news from your Lord is that as the scripture says, Jesus is on your side, and you are still precious to him; when they left you, God remained with you, and He didn't go way or turn his back on you.

Now, for your recovery, start looking at yourself the way God is looking at you. Remove all hate from your heart, the hate you had for those people betrayed you, I mean all those who worked for your downfall, and focus on what God says to your spirit. Be steadfast and focus on your calling. Rise up from inside your heart because the Lord God is on your side. His word says:

The Wounded Soldier

"If the Lord is on our side, who can be against us?"
Hebrew 13:5

The most important quality is to have peace with God in your heart because you are justified through faith. Therefore, the peace with your God through Jesus Christ will shelter you day and night.

"Therefore, since we have been justified through faith,
we have peace with God through our Lord Jesus Christ, through
whom we have gained access by faith into this
grace in which we now stand.
And we boast in the hope of the glory of God.
Not only so, but we also glory in our sufferings, because we know
that suffering produces
perseverance, character, and hope."
Romans 5:1-4

All we have to do is rise up and do it now. Your Lord and Savior is coming back soon, and when He comes, He is going to concentrate on you and what He expects you to do. He will ask you for the talents and the gifts He gave you, and there will be no excuse in mentioning friends who love you or the enemy that betrayed you. Note that these friends have nothing to do with you. They didn't call you; Jesus called you. They didn't save you; Jesus died to save you, and He has been on your side since he saved you and paid the price to set you free.

[2] "Consider it pure joy, my brothers and sisters, whenever you
face trials of many kinds, [3] because you know that the testing of
your faith produces perseverance.
[4] Let perseverance finish its work so that you may be mature and
complete, not lacking anything.

⁵ If any of you lacks wisdom, you should ask God, who gives generously to all without finding fault, and it will be given to you. ⁶ But when you ask, you must believe and not doubt, because the one who doubts is like a wave of the sea, blown and tossed by the wind."
James 1:2-6

This is your time to cry to God like King David. He had a big army of horses and the whole kingdom, but he cried to God because he felt lonely and helpless without God. My friend, in this situation you have been going through, you need Him and only Him

⁷ "Hear my voice when I call, Lord; be merciful to me and answer me. ⁸ My heart says of you, 'Seek his face!' Your face, Lord, I will seek. ⁹ Do not hide your face from me, do not turn your servant away in anger; you have been my helper. Do not reject me or forsake me, God my Savior."
Psalms 27:7-9

My heart says of you, "Seek his face!" Your face, Lord, I will seek.

My friend, the main thing you have to do, which is hard, but you have to do it, is to forgive all your enemies, offload them from your heart, and let them go away. It was made very clear in the word of God: forgive and you will be forgiven.

¹⁴ "For if you forgive other people when they sin against you, your heavenly Father will also forgive you.
¹⁵ But if you do not forgive others their sins, your Father will not forgive your sins."
Mt. 6:14-15

The word of God continues to be clearer to tell you to forgive others as it is very important in our Christianity and our daily life.

¹² "Therefore, as God's chosen people, holy and dearly loved, clothe yourselves with compassion, kindness, humility, gentleness, and patience. ¹³ Bear with each other and forgive one another if any of you has a grievance against someone. Forgive as the Lord forgave you. ¹⁴ And over all these virtues put on love, which binds them all together in perfect unity."
Colossians 3:12-14

You have to see yourself as the chosen one of God and be what the word of God says about you, and you have to check yourself on the list of holy and dearly loved and clothe yourself **with compassion, kindness, humility, gentleness**, and patience, etc.

Therefore, forget whatever they said about you, and you have to ignore every negative noise around you because that noise has nothing to do with what the Lord is doing in your life. The loud noise around you may be praising you or mocking you. Your God is the one who has the final word. Remember, the Lord expects you to do something you didn't do when you were attacked. He needs you to do it now for Him in these last evil days.

All fake stories they told about you are deleted, and all the snares they set for your downfall are no more, and the burden they put on your back is now off. The tears have been wiped away from your eyes. Forget the past when all these happened, when there was nobody to stand with you, and nobody understood what you went through. This time, you know and understand that you are not alone. God is with you.

Let us have the true example of Hannah in book of 1 Samuel. Today, we have many believers who are going through tires and pain like Hannah. They have problems in their private life, and they cry to the Lord day and night, and nobody even wants to know the full story, and the little people do know, they criticize them for it.

Hannah's problem was that she had no child, and her rival, Peninnah, and her friends kept provoking and mocking her in order to irritate her until she cried day and night in prayer. Nobody understood what Hannah was going through. In verse 10, the bible says, "In bitterness of soul, Hannah wept much and prayed to the Lord."

But the matter was made worse in verses 12-13, when Hannah was praying, and Eli observed her mouth moving, but her voice was not heard. Hannah thought maybe God was going to give her a prophecy about her getting a baby, but Eli thought Hannah was drunk, and Eli rebuked her, "How long will you keep on getting drunk? Get rid of your wine.

Even with Hannah's tears, this man of God had no idea what was going on with Hannah. In Eli's mind, Hannah was drunk all the time, not praying. So don't blame yourself and don't take people's words because like Eli, they don't know what is going on. Our Lord Jesus said it on the cross: "Father, forgive them because they don't know what they do."

⁶ "Because the Lord had closed Hannah's womb, her rival kept provoking her in order to irritate her. ⁷ This went on year after year. Whenever Hannah went up to the house of the Lord, her rival provoked her till she wept and would not eat. ⁸ Her husband Elkanah would say to her, 'Hannah, why are you weeping? Why don't you eat? Why are you downhearted? Don't I mean more to you than ten sons?"

⁹ Once when they had finished eating and drinking in Shiloh, Hannah stood up. Now Eli the priest was sitting on his chair by the doorpost of the Lord's house. ¹⁰ In her deep anguish Hannah prayed to the Lord, weeping bitterly.

¹¹ And she made a vow, saying, 'Lord Almighty, if you will only look on your servant's misery and remember me, and not forget your servant but give her a son, then I will give him to the Lord for all the days of his life, and no razor will ever be used on his head.'

¹² As she kept on praying to the Lord, Eli observed her mouth. ¹³ Hannah was praying in her heart, and her lips were moving but her voice was not heard. Eli thought she was drunk ¹⁴ and said to her, 'How long are you going to stay drunk? Put away your wine.'

¹⁵ 'Not so, my lord,' Hannah replied, 'I am a woman who is deeply troubled. I have not been drinking wine or beer; I was pouring out my soul to the Lord.

¹⁶ Do not take your servant for a wicked woman; I have been praying here out of my great anguish and grief.'"
1 Samuel 1:6-16

Today, you might be completely down in fear, but you feel you are ready to rise up again, and you feel God is with you, but have no strength to do anything. You are saying to yourself that you have no more friends to stand with and don't know where to start from because you have been hiding yourself from everybody because no one trusted you. Yes, it is true, you feel you are lost, and you have no strength, and you think nobody trusts you anymore. At this point, you don't need friends, and you don't need people to trust and stand with you. You have to rise up from inside your heart, and you need to hear what the Lord God is telling you.

Another good example is Gideon in the book of Judges when the Medians oppressed Israel. The Israelites were very much oppressed that they didn't have any right to their crops or food they cooked. At this time, Gideon was hiding under an oak in Ophrah, for he was full of fear of the Medians. He was in the same state as you are. Gideon did not believe in himself, and nobody trusted him to do anything about the Medians. That is why when angel told him, "The Lord is with you, mighty warrior." Gideon reacted and asked the angel many challenging questions. When you put all of it together, the questions and explanations, Gideon seemed to be wondering whether the angel knew what he was talking about. But the angel insisted because he was sent to deliver the massage. He didn't care about Gideon's reasons:

^{11} "The angel of the Lord came and sat down under the oak in Ophrah that belonged to Joash the Abiezrite, where his son Gideon was threshing wheat in a winepress to keep it from the Midianites.
^{12} When the angel of the Lord appeared to Gideon, he said, 'The Lord is with you, mighty warrior.'
^{13} 'Pardon me, my lord,' Gideon replied, 'but if the Lord is with us, why has all this happened to us? Where are all his wonders that our ancestors told us about when they said, did not the Lord bring us up out of Egypt? But now the Lord has abandoned us and given us into the hand of Median.'
^{14} The Lord turned to him and said, 'Go in the strength you have and save Israel out of Median's hand. Am I not sending you?'

> ¹⁵ *'Pardon me, my lord,' Gideon replied, 'but how can I save Israel? My clan is the weakest in Manasseh, and I am the least in my family.'*
> ¹⁶ *The Lord answered, 'I will be with you, and you will strike down all the Midianites, leaving none alive.'"*
> *Judges 6:11-16*

As God was with Gideon, He is with you the same. Put aside your fear and hear what the Lord is telling you. Rise up again in strength and serve Him. He is sending you, and He will be with you. You need His word first. You don't need to get advice from people before you hear what God saying.

Since our Lord Jesus is coming much sooner than you expect, this is the only opportunity to act before he shows up, so clean up your way and organize your life. Let your wounds heal quickly, and do something from what He called you to do, for He is coming with your reward.

It is high time you should not go by the words of people because the bible tells us that some people are like Pharisees who tie heavy burdens to other people that they cannot carry, and everything they do is done for people to see, without actual care for anybody.

> ² *"The teachers of the law and the Pharisees sit in Moses' seat. ³ So you must be careful to do everything they tell you. But do not do what they do, for they do not practice what they preach. ⁴ They tie up heavy, cumbersome loads and put them on other people's shoulders, but they themselves are not willing to lift a finger to move them.*
> ⁵ *"Everything they do is done for people to see: They make their phylacteries[.] **wide and the tassels on their***

garments long; *⁶ they love the place of honor at banquets and the most important seats in the synagogues."*
Matthew 23:2-6

And you have to know the truth of who you are in the Lord, our God, because in Him we live and move and have our bearing, for he said that we are his offspring, which is contrary to how people talk about us.

²⁸ "For in him we live and move and have our being.' As some of your own poets have said, 'We are his offspring.'
²⁹ Therefore since we are God's offspring, we should not think that the divine being is like gold or silver or stone—an image made by human design and skill."
Acts 17:28-29

When you understand all these words from your God, you'll finally be strong and live a worthy life. As our Lord Jesus Christ went through suffering for our sake, He wants you to join Him like a soldier, as we have already seen, and we have our commanding officer fighting on our side. Therefore, be strong in the Lord, as the scriptures said:

³ "Join with me in suffering,
like a good soldier of Christ Jesus.
⁴ No one serving as a soldier gets entangled in civilian affairs, but rather tries to please his commanding officer. ⁵ Similarly, anyone who competes as an athlete does not receive the victor's crown except by competing according to the rules.
⁶ The hardworking farmer should be the first to receive a share of the crops.
⁷ Reflect on what I am saying, for the Lord will give you insight into all this.

⁸ Remember Jesus Christ, raised from the dead, and descended from David. This is my gospel, ⁹ for which I am suffering even to the point of being chained like a criminal. But God's word is not chained."
2 Tim. 2:3-8

Therefore, suffering is part of our calling, as Timothy said that he was like a criminal in his suffering. You need to know that you are not alone going through this type of situation, and your Lord knows everything about you.

My friend, you need to know from today how much Jesus Christ our Lord cares for you. He can't pass by you or leave you alone to die from your wounds.

And if you were wounded like the man who was going down from Jerusalem and was attacked by robbers, wounded, and left half dead, with everybody passing by him without a care. But as God had planned, the good Samaritan came to take care of this man, and God still has a plan for taking care of you. God has planned this book for you, as good Samaritan, to take care of your wounds; that is why you have to take a very serious stand of spiritual life now, as you read from this book. For it is time for your healing.

"A man was going down from Jerusalem to Jericho, when he was attacked by robbers. They stripped him of his clothes, beat him and went away, leaving him half dead. A priest happened to be going down the same road, and when he saw the man, he passed by on the other side.
So too, a Levite, when he came to the place and saw him, passed by on the other side. But a Samaritan, as he traveled, came where the man was; and when he saw him, he took pity on him. He went to him and bandaged his wounds, pouring on oil and wine.

Then he put the man on his own donkey, brought him to an inn and took care of him.
The next day he took out two denarii and gave them to the innkeeper. 'Look after him,' he said, 'and when I return, I will reimburse you for any extra expense you may have.'"
Luke 10:30-35

And if you were left in a pit like Joseph when his brothers throw him into that pit, like garbage with no value, and you too thought you have no value, God has set aside those to buy you with value so that you continue to your destination of success.

You have to rise up again and start bearing fruits from the gifts God gave you from the beginning and become powerful according to his might and glorify his name.

[10] "So that you may live a life worthy of the Lord and please him in every way: bearing fruit in every good work, growing in the knowledge of God,
[11] being strengthened with all power according to his glorious might so that you may have great endurance and patience, [12] and giving joyful thanks to the Father,
who has qualified you to share in the inheritance of his holy people in the kingdom of light."
Colossians 1:10-12

Since the Lord said in his word that he is coming back soon, and He is coming with your reward, that is why you have to work hard in this remaining time - so that you don't miss your reward.

[12] "Look, I am coming soon! My reward is with me, and I will give to each person according to what they have done. [13] I am the

Alpha and the Omega, the First and the Last, the Beginning and the End.
¹⁴ Blessed are those who wash their robes, that they may have the right to the tree of life and may go through the gates into the city."
Revelation 22:12-14

This is your time to fill up your lamp with enough oil for yourself, like the wise virgins, before the door is closed because if it closes before you fill up your lamp, you will be left out like the five foolish virgins. As the word of God says, keep watch because you do not know the day or the hour. Today is your day to do it.

"At that time the kingdom of heaven will be like ten virgins who took their lamps and went out to meet the bridegroom. ² Five of them were foolish and five were wise. ³ The foolish ones took their lamps but did not take any oil with them. ⁴ The wise ones, however, took oil in jars along with their lamps. ⁵ The bridegroom was a long time in coming, and they all became drowsy and fell asleep.
⁶ At midnight the cry rang out:
'Here's the bridegroom! Come out to meet him!'
⁷ Then all the virgins woke up and trimmed their lamps. ⁸ The foolish ones said to the wise, 'Give us some of your oil; our lamps are going out.'
⁹ 'No,' they replied, 'there may not be enough for both us and you. Instead, go to those who sell oil and buy some for yourselves.'
¹⁰ But while they were on their way to buy the oil, the bridegroom arrived. The virgins who were ready went in with him to the wedding banquet. And the door was shut.

¹¹ Later the others also came. 'Lord, Lord,' they said, 'open the door for us!'

¹² But he replied, 'Truly I tell you, I don't know you.
¹³ Therefore keep watch, because you do not know the day or the hour.'"
Matthew 25:1-13

This is your time to change your history and your future; you have to be a winner and be victorious in all areas of your life because the battle belongs to the Lord.

²¹ "To the one who is victorious, I will give the right to sit with me on my throne, just as I was victorious and sat down with my Father on his throne. ²² Whoever has ears, let them hear what the Spirit says to the churches."
Revelation 3:21-22

After applying all of the healing word of God to your life, the healing takes place from then on and at every moment you do what the word of God says. And above of all, you are reconciled with your heavenly Father. In this process, you become a brand new person with a brand new life.

⁸ "But God demonstrates his own love for us in this:
While we were still sinners, Christ died for us.
⁹ Since we have now been justified by his blood,

how much more shall we be saved from God's wrath through him!

¹⁰ For if, while we were God's enemies, we were reconciled to him through the death of his Son, how much more, having been reconciled, shall we be saved through his life!
¹¹ Not only is this so, but we also boast in God through our Lord Jesus Christ, through whom we have now received reconciliation."

The Wounded Soldier

My friend, this is the time for you to clean up every mess, as the word says it clearly in the bible.
¹⁴ "Blessed are those who wash their robes, that they may have the right to the tree of life and may go through the gates into the city."
Revelation 22:14

And when you feel in your heart that you have received the reconciliation with your heavenly Father, please start doing what he had called you to do. Imagine this, Jesus Christ our Savior chose Saul among so many people to be his servant, yet Saul was killing Christians and persecuting the disciples and all other believers.

Now, my friend, the present is overtime. It is like when it is game over, and the referee gives extra time. This is the time you have left to make a difference between life and death. Just do His work without ceasing, bear fruits as much as possible, and let His name be glorified through your life. He is going to do new things in your life.

Remember now, you are God's chosen person. Therefore, fight your good fight of faith as a holy and gifted person, full of gifts of the Holy Spirit. As you continue forgiving those who attack you, the Lord keeps forgiving you day by day. Don't forget to work in unity with the body of Christ.

¹² "Therefore, as God's chosen people, holy and dearly loved, clothe yourselves with compassion, kindness, humility, gentleness and patience.
¹³ Bear with each other and forgive one another
if any of you has a grievance against someone.
Forgive as the Lord forgave you.
¹⁴ And over all these virtues put on love,
which binds them all together in perfect unity."
Colossians 3:12-17

At this moment, you are receiving your deliverance and your healing from all the pain of your wounds; listen to the word of God and let the peace of God rule your heart without fear, for you are a member of one body of Christ, and you were called to peace.

[15] "Let the peace of Christ rule in your hearts, since as members of one body you were called to peace. And be thankful.
[16] Let the message of Christ dwell among you richly as you teach and admonish one another with all wisdom through psalms, hymns, and songs from the Spirit, singing to God with gratitude in your hearts.
[17] And whatever you do, whether in word or deed, do it all in the name of the Lord Jesus, giving thanks to God the Father through him."

Remember, God has put you together in a certain way, on purpose and for a purpose; therefore, don't spend more time fighting with people or trying to change who God created in you. Please ignore the past and focus on God's gift and calling - they are still alive, residing within you.

Therefore, be thankful that you were not left alone, wounded and chained by the enemy. Now that you are blessed, please pass this book over to someone you know who needs healing from the same type of situations, and God will add more blessings on you,

Be realistic as you think about your current state. Then, look at the change that God wants to do in your life through faith. A limited faith means a limited future.

The main question you have to ask yourself now after recovering and restored is that: What miracles might God want me to do in my life that would show the whole earth that there is a God in the land and bring back God's Glory.

www.ingramcontent.com/pod-product-compliance
Lightning Source LLC
LaVergne TN
LVHW020430080526
838202LV00055B/5107